T0052718

WORLD WINDOWS

A Savings Plan

HEINLE CENGAGE Learning™

Y|S|G A YBM COMPANY Young & Son Global, Inc.

How do you save money?
£10
Bank of England
TEN
Pounds
MAMPUNG PISO
UNITED STATES OF AMERICA
WASHINGTON D.C.
港幣
By order of the Board

Contents

Vocabulary	4	On Thursday	11
Lisa's Problem	6	On Friday	12
On Sunday	7	On Saturday	13
On Monday	8	Summary	14
On Tuesday	9	Social Studies Skill	15
On Wednesday	10	Glossary and Index	16

Vocabulary

chores

earn

rake

laundry

Lisa's Problem

Lisa's friend Brian is going to have a birthday party on Saturday.

Lisa wants to buy Brian a book that costs seven dollars.

She only has three dollars.

On Sunday

Lisa makes a savings plan.
Every day, she will do chores to earn money.
If she saves the money, she will have
enough money to buy the book.

On Monday

Lisa washes the dishes.
Her mother gives her one dollar.
She puts the money in her piggy bank.

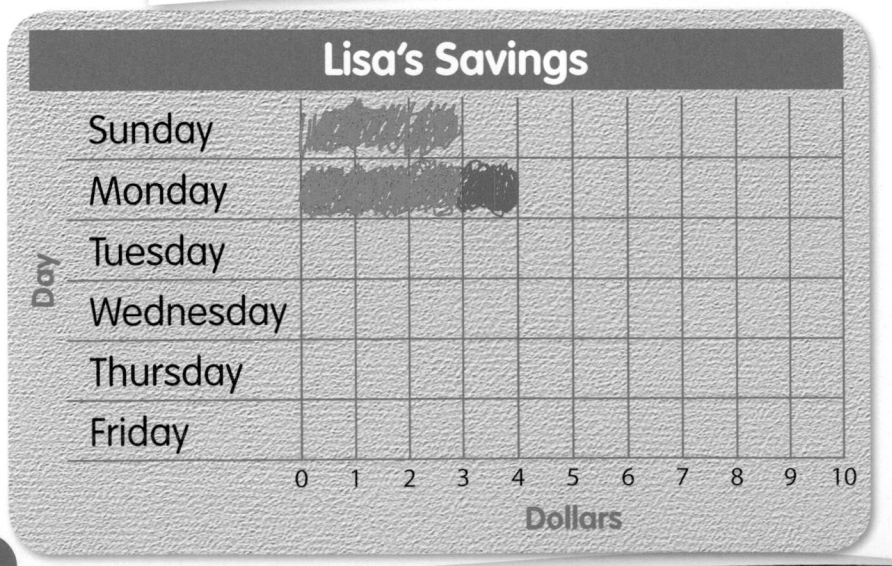

On Tuesday

Lisa takes out the trash in the evening. She earns one more dollar.

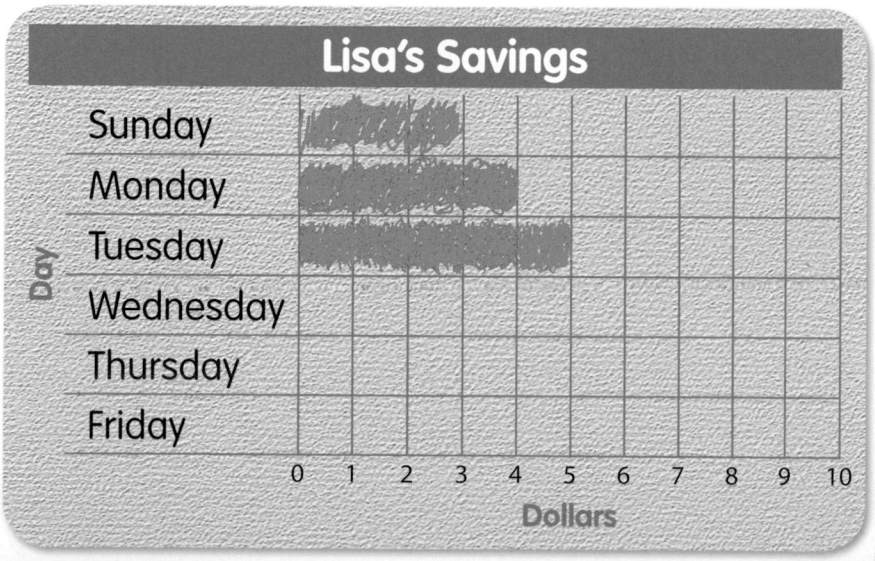

On Wednesday

Lisa's neighbor asks her to rake the leaves.
He gives her three dollars.
Lisa uses one dollar to buy a lollipop.

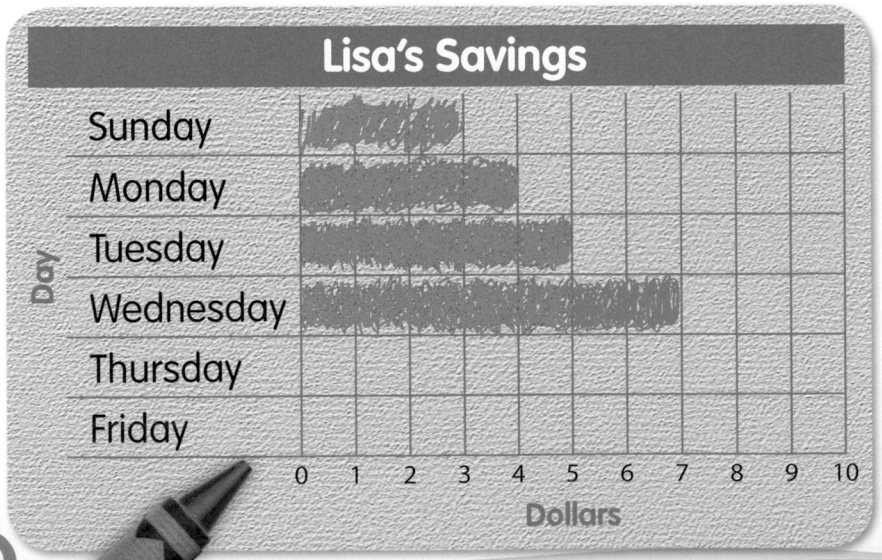

On Thursday

Lisa does the laundry.
She earns two more dollars for doing a good job.

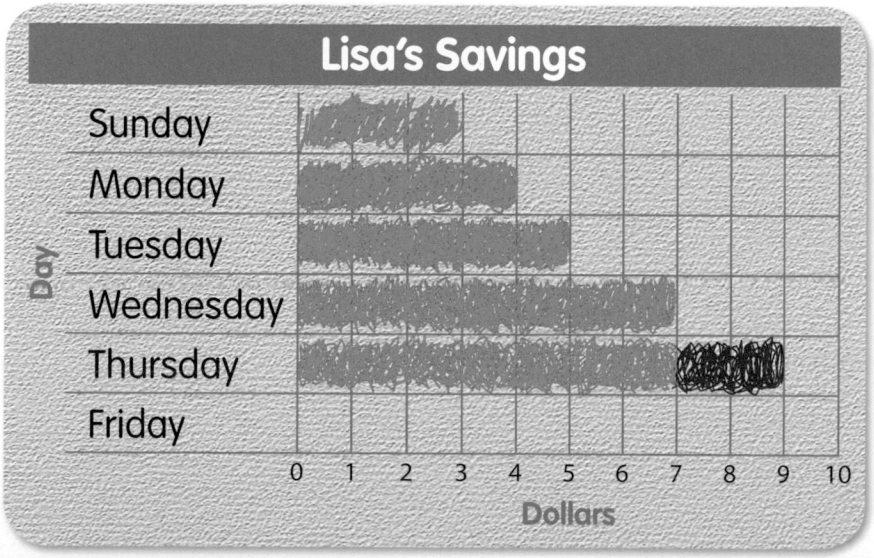

On Friday

Lisa takes all the money out of her piggy bank.
She has nine dollars.
Now she can buy the book!

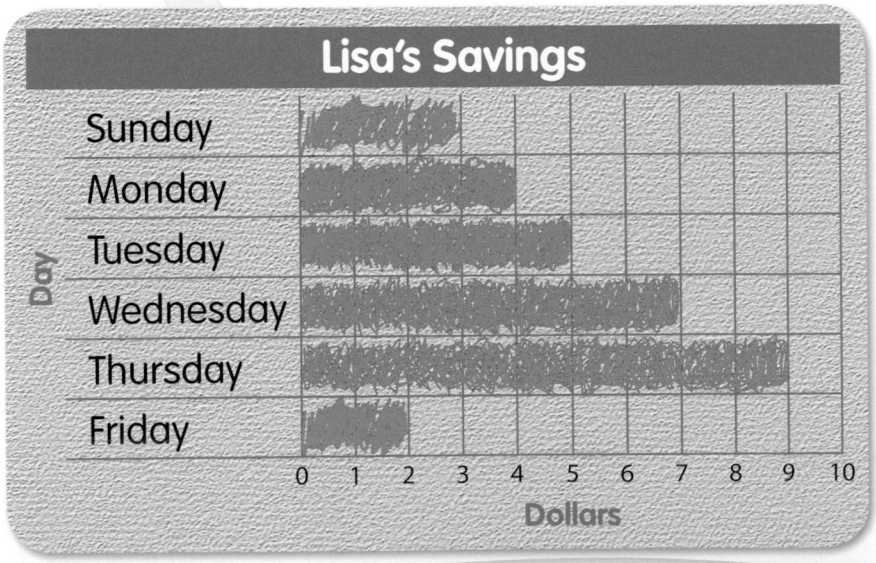

On Saturday

Lisa gives Brian the book and wishes him a happy birthday.
Her plan worked!

Summary

What does Lisa do to earn money?

Social Studies Skill

Read a Bar Graph

A **bar graph** uses bars to compare amounts or numbers of things.

1. On which day does Lisa have four dollars?
2. How much money does Lisa have on Wednesday?
3. On which day does Lisa have the most money?

Glossary

chore
A small job that needs to be done regularly

earn
To get money for work that you do

neighbor
Someone who lives near you

plan
Something that you intend to do and have prepared for

problem
Something that causes trouble or difficulty

save
To keep something, especially money, for use in the future

Index

birthday, 6, 13
chores, 7
dollars, 6, 8–12
earn, 7, 9, 11
Friday, 12
laundry, 11
Monday, 8
money, 7–8, 12
neighbor, 10
piggy bank, 8, 12
plan, 7, 13
rake, 10
Saturday, 6, 13
saves, 7
Sunday, 7
Thursday, 11
Tuesday, 9
Wednesday, 10